LINKING THE PAST AND PRESENT

WHAT DID THE
ANCIENT
EGYPTIANS
DO FOR ME?

Patrick Catel

Heinemann Library
Chicago, Illinois

923
CAT

www.heinemannraintree.com
Visit our website to find out
more information about
Heinemann-Raintree books.

To order:
☎ Phone 888-454-2279
💻 Visit www.heinemannraintree.com
to browse our catalog and order online.

© 2011 Heinemann Library
an imprint of Capstone Global Library, LLC
Chicago, Illinois

Edited by Megan Cotugno and Laura Knowles
Designed by Richard Parker
Original illustrations © Capstone Global Library Limited 2010
Illustrated by Roger@KJA-artists.com
Picture research by Hannah Taylor
Originated by Capstone Global Library Limited
Printed and bound in China by CTPS

14 13 12 11 10
10 9 8 7 6 5 4 3 2 1

Library of Congress Cataloging-in-Publication Data
Catel, Patrick.
  What did the ancient Egyptians do for me? / Patrick Catel.
    p. cm. -- (Linking the past and present)
  Includes bibliographical references and index.
  ISBN 978-1-4329-3742-3 (hc) -- ISBN 978-1-4329-3749-2
(pb) 1. Egypt--Civilization--To 332 B.C.--Juvenile literature.
2. Civilization, Modern--Ancient influences--Juvenile
literature. I. Title.
  DT61.C345 2011
  932--dc22
                        2009039658

Acknowledgments

The author and publisher are grateful to the following for
permission to reproduce copyright material: Alamy Images
pp. 7 (© Middle East), 14 (© Ivy Close Images); Corbis pp. 9
(Daniella Nowitz), 10 (Bettmann), 19 (Reuters/Abed Omar
Qusini), 25 (Robert Harding World Imagery/Yadid Levy);
Getty Images p. 17 (China Photos); istockphoto p. 21 (© Jason
Walton); Photolibrary pp. 13 (Moodboard), 23 (J. D. Dallet);
Rex Features p. 27 (Dan Callister).

Cover photograph of the pyramids of Giza, Egypt, in a desert
landscape reproduced with permission of Getty Images/The
Image Bank/Frans Lemmens.

We would like to thank Dr. Martin Bommas for his invaluable
help in the preparation of this book.

Contents

Look for the Then and Now boxes. They highlight parts of ancient Egyptian culture that are present in our modern world.

Any words appearing in the text in bold, **like this**, are explained in the glossary.

What Did the Ancient Egyptians Do for Me?

The pyramids of Egypt are famous for being one of the seven wonders of the world. They remind us of a great society from long ago. That ancient Egyptian society has passed into history, but we still use some ancient Egyptian inventions, and we do many of the same things they did.

Have you ever wondered why there are **monuments** all around the world shaped like tall, pointed columns? Perhaps you have a pet cat? Do you like the smell of perfume? Maybe you have seen an advertisement for makeup and wondered why people wear it. Do you know how people kept time without clocks and watches? Or how they knew when it was a holiday?

Look at the illustration to the right. Can you see something the ancient Egyptians built that still exists today?

Who Were the Ancient Egyptians?

Ancient Egyptian culture would not have been possible without the waters of the Nile River. The river gave the Egyptians water to drink and to use in farming. This meant they could feed many people. As a result, a great **civilization** was born.

The southern part of Egypt is often called Upper Egypt, and the northern part is called Lower Egypt. It might help to think of the Nile River flowing first through Upper Egypt and then Lower Egypt, as it flows toward the Mediterranean Sea.

The Nile River

The Nile River begins in the southern half of Africa and flows north for hundreds of miles. It passes through Egypt on its way to the Mediterranean Sea. About 160 kilometers (100 miles) before the Nile reaches the Mediterranean, it spreads out into different branches. This is called the Nile **Delta**. The soil of the Nile Delta is excellent for farming.

The Nile River floods every year. The ancient Egyptians used the floodwater for **irrigation**, which is a way of watering crops. Farmers were able to grow plenty of food to feed a growing population. With extra food available, some people did not have to farm. They could spend their time as scholars and artists. They also invented new, improved ways of doing things.

The ancient Egyptians invented one of the world's first written languages, in which they used symbols called **hieroglyphs**. This helped them to organize workers and farming, keep records of population and food, collect taxes, and run a government.

Thousands of Egyptian workers were needed to build **monuments**, such as the Great Pyramid and Sphinx of Giza.

The Nile

The Nile River is the longest river in the world. It is 6,695 kilometers (4,184 miles) long.

Pharaohs

The rulers of ancient Egypt were called the pharaohs. The people believed pharaohs were gods. The three great ages in ancient Egyptian history are called the Old (2686–2181 BCE), Middle (2055–1650 BCE), and New (1550–1069 BCE) Kingdoms. Several different pharaohs ruled during the years of each kingdom. Following each kingdom there were times of unrest or invasion, known as Intermediate Periods.

What Was Ancient Egyptian Art and Architecture Like?

The first pyramid was made for the pharaoh Djoser almost 5,000 years ago. The most famous pyramid, the Great Pyramid, was finished about 4,500 years ago and was 147 meters (481 feet) high. It was made from 2.3 million blocks of limestone. Most blocks weighed about 2.5 tonnes (2.8 tons) each.

Egyptian artists

Ancient Egyptian artists painted colorful scenes on the walls of **tombs**, temples, and houses. Sculptors made statues of pharaohs, gods, and goddesses. Over time, these sculptors began to make the people in their works look more and more real. The ancient Greeks used and built on that knowledge in their own art.

Cleopatra

Cleopatra was the last pharaoh before Roman rule began in Egypt. Her story has been told over and over again, in plays, books, and movies. William Shakespeare, one of the greatest playwrights in history, wrote a play about her called *Antony and Cleopatra*.

THEN...

The ideas of ancient Egyptian art spread around the world. They influenced the ancient Greeks. The ancient Greeks influenced the ancient Romans. The Romans spread these ideas across their empire in Europe, Africa, the Middle East, and western and southern Asia. The Great Pyramid and Sphinx of Giza became famous, along with other Egyptian constructions and art. At times, Egyptian works were so popular that other countries took them out of Egypt to display them back home.

Ancient Egyptian influence can be seen in some modern structures. The entrance to the Louvre Museum in Paris, France, looks like a glass pyramid.

...NOW

The **murals**, statues, and **monuments** in our modern cities are not so different from those of ancient Egypt. Some modern cities have original Egyptian works. **Obelisks** called "Cleopatra's Needles" were removed from Egypt during the 1800s and are now found in London, New York City, and Paris. More recent monuments have also been designed like Egyptian obelisks. The pyramid shape is also found in modern buildings. The modern glass entrance to the Louvre Museum in Paris takes its shape from an Egyptian pyramid.

Egyptian stone

The ancient Egyptians needed to **quarry** stone for their building projects. Quarrying means cutting stone out of a rocky pit in the ground. We still have quarries today, but our machinery makes the job much easier. The ancient Egyptians only had stone and metal tools such as saws, chisels, and wedges.

This illustration shows the Pharos Lighthouse in Alexandria. The lighthouse was a famous tourist attraction and survived for around 1,500 years.

THEN...

Ancient Egyptian buildings included more than just pyramids and temples. The first lighthouse, called the Pharos Lighthouse, was built in Alexandria in northern Egypt. When completed around 270 BCE, the lighthouse was more than 110 meters (350 feet) tall. This is as tall as a 40-story building in our modern world! A bright fire burned at the top of the lighthouse. A large mirror focused the light from the fire into a beam that could warn ships and send signals.

The workers cut out a large piece of rock, then placed it onto a kind of heavy sled. They pushed and pulled the sled to the Nile River. The stone was then taken down the river to the building site. This was repeated many times. It took years to complete a project.

Wonders of the ancient world

The Great Pyramid at Giza is the oldest of the seven wonders of the ancient world. This is a list of some of the most amazing structures and places made by people who lived around the Mediterranean Sea and in the Middle East in ancient times. The Great Pyramid is the only one that still exists. The others included the Hanging Gardens of Babylon, the statue of Zeus at Olympia, and the Pharos Lighthouse of Alexandria.

...NOW

The Pharos Lighthouse was one of the wonders of the ancient world. Tourists even visited it. For hundreds of years, people built lighthouses on coasts around the world. They helped ships avoid rocks and safely approach the coast. And today we build 40-story structures and buildings even taller, called skyscrapers. The Pharos Lighthouse of ancient Egypt was like a skyscraper of the ancient world!

What Was Life Like in Ancient Egypt?

The ancient Egyptians used many clever inventions in their daily lives. They made musical instruments such as harps and flutes. They built boats and invented the sail, which allowed them to travel quickly up and down the Nile River. They also invented a kind of lock with a bolt and key, called a tumbler lock, that allowed people to protect their homes. The folding stool, another Egyptian invention, was a common piece of furniture.

Daily life

Adults in ancient Egypt played board games to pass the time. Children had toys, including dolls, toy boats, and toy animals that had moving parts. People usually wore plain, white clothing, but the wealthy sometimes wore colorful robes, dresses, and wigs. Ancient Egyptians also wore jewelry and makeup.

Egyptian cosmetics
Today, we know that lead is poisonous, but the ancient Egyptians used it in their makeup!

THEN...

Both rich and poor, and men and women, used perfume and makeup in ancient Egypt. Makeup was made from ground-up **minerals**, plants, and herbs that were mixed with fat and oil from nuts and fruits. The ancient Egyptians even applied makeup to **mummies**. It was thought to be important to make a good impression on the gods after death.

...NOW

Makeup today is made from similar materials. Like the ancient Egyptians, the most wealthy and famous people today have experts to apply their makeup for them. People who work in **mortuaries** today sometimes apply makeup to the dead, so that the last time people see them they look their best.

This is a painting of a wild cat found on the wall of an Egyptian **tomb**. The cats we keep as pets today are descendants of the African wild cats the Egyptians tamed thousands of years ago.

THEN...

The ancient Egyptians were the first people to domesticate the cat as a popular pet. At first, cats were just useful for controlling mice and other pests. Later, they were **worshipped** and were often given gold jewelry to wear. They were so respected that when they died, they were often mummified, just like their owners!

Clocks and calendars

The ancient Egyptians used a calendar that is similar to ours. There were 12 months in a year, with 30 days each. There were also an extra 5 days added at the end of the year, to make 365 days in total. This calendar was based on the movements of the sun, which was studied by **astronomers**. Egyptians enjoyed many festivals and celebrations every year. Most festivals were religious. The times when festivals took place were based on the cycles of the moon.

Ancient Egyptian clocks, on the other hand, were quite different from ours. They used water clocks, which were containers filled with water. There were special markings on the inside and a hole near the bottom. As the water slowly leaked out, the markings would show what time it was.

Egyptian sports

The ancient Egyptians enjoyed sports. They played a lot of games that we can recognize today, such as ball games, races, and wrestling. They also took part in activities such as javelin throwing, archery, swimming, rowing, and hunting.

...NOW

Today, cats are kept as pets all over the world. Even though people do not worship them in the same way as the ancient Egyptians, they are some of the most loved pets we own. They are also still very useful to us because they hunt pests. There are about 90 million pet cats in the United States alone!

What Did the Ancient Egyptians Do for Work?

Most people in ancient Egypt were farmers. However, they sometimes had to spend their time working in a trade that was different from their own. Everyone had to pay taxes to the pharaoh, and many people paid their share by working on a building project. They could also be made to join the army.

Some people in ancient Egypt had government jobs. Many **scribes** worked for the government keeping written records, but some were teachers. It was the job of priests and priestesses to look after the temples. Artists decorated **tombs** and temples. Wealthy Egyptians also paid artists to decorate their homes. Some people were servants in the homes of the wealthy. Slaves also did similar work, such as cooking and cleaning. Other workers of ancient Egypt included fishermen, weavers, metal workers, potters, carpenters, boat builders, wig makers, and embalmers.

Daily wages

The daily wage for an Egyptian worker was 10 loaves of bread and up to 2 jugs of beer.

THEN...

Thousands of workers were needed to build pyramids, temples, and **monuments** for the gods and pharaohs. The Great Pyramid at Giza used at least 30,000 workers—and possibly as many as 100,000! This was the first time such a huge workforce was used in human history. There were teams of **architects** and **engineers**, and supervisors and their workers had to understand every task they needed to do. The construction of one pyramid could last dozens of years.

Today, large, organized workforces still construct buildings, but they also build cars and many other products.

...NOW

The idea of organizing large groups of workers for specific tasks changed human history. Modern-day marvels like skyscrapers and suspension bridges would not be possible without large, organized workforces. The machines we use for transportation every day rely on large workforces. It takes hundreds of people to make and ship all the parts that go into a modern car. It then takes more organized workers in an **assembly line** to put the car together.

Canals

The ancient Egyptians built **canals** to carry water from the Nile River to the farms. Local noblemen kept track of how much water each farm received. They wanted to make sure everyone got their fair share.

When the Nile flooded each year, the canals were opened up to allow water to flow to the farms. At the height of the flooding in September, the canals were closed again. When the water level went down, the farmers plowed their fields and planted crops. They were probably the first farmers to use a plow pulled along by animals to turn the soil over before planting.

Canals made watering fields of crops much easier. Otherwise, farmers would have had to carry water from the river.

THEN...

The ancient Egyptians are thought to be the first beekeepers. The Egyptians made hives from woven baskets covered with clay. The hives were then stacked on top of each other. When it was time to harvest the honey and wax, the Egyptians blew smoke into the back of the hives, and the bees flew out the front. Honey was very valuable. Temples kept bees and made offerings of honey to the gods.

This modern beekeeper is wearing protective clothing while she handles a tray of honeycomb. Smoke is still used to help control bees, as it was in ancient Egypt.

King Tut's tomb

The **tomb** of the pharaoh Tutankhamun was opened in 1922. There was some honey inside. If you wanted to, you could still eat it, because honey never goes bad!

...NOW

Today, we harvest honey and wax from kept beehives, much as the Egyptians did. Honey is still a popular sweetener. It is also used in ointments. The ancient Egyptians understood, as we do today, that honey helps heal wounds and fight infection. As Earth's population grew, honeybees became very important for **pollinating** crops around the world. In this way, they play a very important part in feeding the world.

How Were the Ancient Egyptians Educated?

Only the sons of the wealthiest people were educated in ancient Egypt. They learned from **scribes**, tutors, or in schools. They studied reading, writing, math, music, medicine, and **astronomy**. They wrote down their lessons on pieces of pottery.

Girls did not learn any of these skills. Instead, they were taught at home by their mothers. They learned how to cook, clean, care for children, and run a household.

Scribes

Scribes in ancient Egypt were highly respected. They had to memorize over 700 **hieroglyphs**! These symbols were used on the walls of **tombs** and temples. A simpler version of hieroglyphs, called **hieratic writing**, was used for government records and letters. The sons of scribes often became scribes, too.

Hieroglyphs

Hieroglyphs could be written from left to right or right to left. They could be arranged in rows or columns.

THEN...

The word "paper" comes from the papyrus plant. This is a tall reed that grows on the banks of the Nile River. The ancient Egyptians used these reeds to make papyrus paper. This was an important invention. Paper allows people to write down and keep a lot of information, using up little space. It is also light and can be moved around.

These are hieroglyphs. The ancient Egyptians wrote them in long lines, without spaces. Some symbols stand for sounds, and others stand for objects or ideas.

...NOW

Paper has allowed us to pass on information more easily in books, newspapers, and records. It has helped to create a more educated population around the world. Today, most people use paper every day of their lives. However, with the invention of the computer, electronic files now store a lot of records, especially for governments and companies.

What Did the Egyptians Know About Medicine?

Ancient Egyptian healers knew a lot about the human body. They wrote medical books on papyrus that you can still see in museums today. They knew where most of the **organs** in the human body were and what they did. They gave their patients medicines made from plants, herbs, and animal parts. They also performed operations. People came from far away to watch the healers at work.

Embalming

The reason the ancient Egyptians knew so much about the human body was that they were able to study it during **embalming**. This was the method used to make a **mummy**. Embalmers removed the brain of a dead person through his or her nostrils. They cut open the body and took out all its organs. These were all placed in **canopic jars**. The only organ they did not remove was the heart, which they believed was where a person's intelligence was located.

THEN...

To help with embalming and performing operations, the ancient Egyptians used tools such as knives, drills, saws, hooks, and scales. Healers and embalmers also checked dead bodies for the cause of illness or death. They recorded the injuries they treated and the medicines they used to treat them.

The brain

The ancient Egyptians did not understand all the organs. They were not sure what the brain did and simply got rid of it during embalming.

The lids of these canopic jars were carved to show the heads of ancient Egyptian gods.

...NOW

Just like the ancient Egyptians, modern doctors have learned about diseases from dead bodies. If someone has died and the cause is not known, a doctor will perform an autopsy. This is an examination of the dead body, just like those done by the ancient Egyptians.

How Did the Ancient Egyptians Govern?

The pharaoh was the leader of ancient Egypt. After the pharaoh, royal family, and priests came the rest of the nobles, or upper class. This included administrators, military commanders, and **scribes**. Under the pharaoh was the **vizier**. He made sure things ran smoothly and reported to the pharaoh. Other important administrators included the **treasurer**, tax collector, and minister of public works. Then came the majority of Egyptians, who were the peasant farmers.

Peasant farmers could be made to join the army to pay their tax of work. However, the army also contained slaves and **mercenaries**. Slaves in ancient Egypt were usually prisoners captured during war. Mercenaries were hired soldiers. Taxes of food and work supported the temples and priests, as well as the government and military. No one wanted to take the unpopular job of tax collector. We know the ancient Egyptians complained about taxes, just as people do today!

THEN...

At its peak, there were three million people living in ancient Egypt. The pharaoh's government taxed the people in the form of work in order to build the pyramids and other large constructions. The ancient Egyptian government also taxed the people in the form of food, which it then stored. The government gave the food out to people in times of need, to make sure they did not go hungry. This helped the government stay popular and in control.

Bridges such as the Golden Gate Bridge in San Francisco, California, could not have been built without the help of money from taxes.

...NOW

The ancient Egyptians were the first in the western world to tax so many people in such an organized way. Today, taxes make most modern societies possible. However, taxes are now usually paid with money. Governments then use that collected money to pay for services and construction projects. We expect more from our governments today, including education, police and fire protection, and other services.

Ancient Egyptian justice

Ancient Egyptians developed their idea of justice from their religion. The goddess Ma'at represented truth, justice, order, and balance in the universe. The pharaoh was the supreme judge lawmaker. However, other government officials dealt with most matters of law and justice. Anyone could go to court to have complaints heard, but peasants were probably not treated as well as wealthy people in the ancient Egyptian legal system.

The ancient Egyptians did not have police as we do today. During the New Kingdom period (1550–1069 BCE) a group called the *medjay* acted as guards. They also investigated crimes. Punishments in ancient Egypt were severe. Sometimes the *medjay* punished criminals with beatings and torture. Other punishments included being banished, or being forced to do dangerous work in mines or **quarries**. In some cases, a criminal might be whipped or even have a body part, such as the nose, cut off!

The death penalty

Only the pharaoh was allowed to sentence someone to death. Sometimes he would offer the criminal the choice between being executed or committing suicide.

THEN...

Ancient Egyptians argued over land and water. They were quick to take their arguments to court, as people often are today. The most important cases brought to the ancient Egyptian courts were passed on to the pharaoh to decide. Although punishments could be harsh, it was rare for someone to be sentenced to death. The ancient Egyptians kept records of past cases and used them to decide future ones.

Modern police forces keep order, as the *medjay* did in ancient Egypt.

...NOW

Today, the idea that anyone can seek out justice in a legal system is considered an important part of a modern society. We still use the outcome of past cases to reach a decision about a current case. This is called using precedent. We also sometimes refer a case from a lower court to a higher court, just as the ancient Egyptians did. There are some countries around the world that still sentence some criminals to death.

Key Dates

Here is an outline of the different periods in the history of ancient Egypt, and the important moments in its history and culture that happened during these times:

around 5500–3100 BCE

Predynastic Period
Earliest evidence of **hieroglyphic** writing

Irrigation is used to increase the amount of land used for farming

Sails are added to boats, allowing Egyptians to use wind to travel up the Nile River more easily

3100–2686 BCE

Early Dynastic Period
Upper and Lower Egypt are joined into one kingdom

Papyrus is used as a writing surface

The first calendar is developed, based on the movements of the sun and solar system

2686–2181 BCE

Old Kingdom
The first pyramid, called the Step Pyramid, is built for King Djoser. It is built using the organized labor of many workers.

The world's first true pyramid, with smooth sides, is built

King Khufu's Great Pyramid of Giza is built

Record-keeping of goods occurs

Ox-drawn plows are used for farming

2181–2055 BCE	**First Intermediate Period** Provinces within Egypt are independently governed
2055–1650 BCE	**Middle Kingdom** Earliest evidence of healers using the practice of medicine to diagnose illnesses
1650–1550 BCE	**Second Intermediate Period** Period of unrest and foreign rule by the Hyksos, who were originally from Asia
1550–1069 BCE	**New Kingdom** Reign of the female pharaoh Hatshepsut Reign of Tutankhamun
1069–747 BCE	**Third Intermediate Period** Period of foreign rule by the Nubians, who came from an area of Africa south of Egypt
747–332 BCE	**Late Period** The Persians, who were originally from Asia, conquer Egypt
332 BCE– 395 CE	**Greek-Roman Period** Alexander the Great invades Egypt Alexander the Great founds the city of Alexandria Roman rule begins in Egypt

Glossary

architect person whose job it is to design buildings

assembly line system of making things in a factory where products move past a line of workers, who each put together or check one specific part of the product

astronomer person who studies the stars and planets

canal long passage dug into the ground and filled with water

canopic jar jar used in ancient Egypt to contain the organs of a mummy

civilization society that has developed high levels of organization and government, art, writing, medicine, and other cultural accomplishments

delta mouth of a river, where it splits into several parts, flowing into the sea

embalm treat a dead body with substances to keep it from rotting

engineer person whose job it is to design or build structures such as machines or bridges

hieratic writing Egyptian writing used for everyday purposes, such as letters and keeping records

hieroglyphs Egyptian picture symbols that represented sounds that made up words

irrigation supplying land or crops with water

mercenary soldier hired to serve in a foreign army

mineral substance formed in the earth, such as gold or salt, that can be dug out and used

monument statue, building, or other structure, sometimes built to remember a person or event

mortuary also called a funeral home; place where the dead are prepared for burial

mummy dead body that has been embalmed and wrapped in cloth

mural picture that is painted on a wall inside or outside a building

obelisk tall stone pillar with a pyramid-shaped top, built as a reminder of an event or person

organ part of the body that does a particular job, such as the heart or lungs

pollinate put pollen from a male flower onto the female part of a plant, so that fruit and seeds begin to form

quarry place where large amounts of stone are dug out of the ground; also, to dig stone out of a quarry

scribe person in ancient Egypt whose job it was to write or to teach others to write

tomb underground burial place, often with a monument built on the ground above it

treasurer person who is in charge of the money of a government or organization

vizier very important official

worship praising and showing respect for a god, gods, or animals or people seen as gods. It may involve singing, praying, and other ways of showing respect.

Find Out More

Books

Harris, Nathaniel. *Clues to the Past: Everyday Life in Ancient Egypt*. Mankato, Minn.: Sea-to-Sea, 2006.

Hart, George. *Eyewitness: Ancient Egypt*. New York: Dorling Kindersley, 2008.

Rees, Rosemary. *Understanding People in the Past: The Ancient Egyptians*. Chicago: Heinemann Library, 2007.

Websites

http://egypt.mrdonn.org
This website has lots of information on the history and everyday life of the ancient Egyptians.

www.carnegiemnh.org/exhibitions/egypt/index.htm
This website has lots of information about ancient Egypt.

www.historyforkids.org/learn/egypt
Find out more about ancient Egyptian food, religion, games, clothes, and much more on this useful website.

Index